cloverleaf books™

My Healthy Habits

Move Your Body!

My Exercise Tips

Gina Bellisario

illustrated by Renée Kurilla

M MILLBROOK PRESS · MINNEAPOLIS

For Milla, my bug girl—G.B.

For my husband, Keith, the best
teammate—R.K.

Millbrook Press
A division of Lerner Publishing Group, Inc.
241 First Avenue North
Minneapolis, MN 55401 U.S.A.

For reading levels and more information, look up this title at
www.lernerbooks.com.

Main body text set in Slappy Inline 18/28.
Typeface provided by T26.

Library of Congress Cataloging-in-Publication Data

Bellisario, Gina.
     Move Your Body! / by Gina Bellisario ; illustrated by Renée
Kurilla.
       pages   cm. — (Cloverleaf books. basic health habits)
     Includes index.
     ISBN 978-1-4677-1349-8 (lib. bdg. : alk. paper)
     ISBN 978-1-4677-2535-4 (eBook)
     1. Exercise—Juvenile literature. 2. Physical fitness—Juvenile
literature. I. Kurilla, Renée, illustrator. II. Title.
RA781.B398 2014
613.7'1—dc23   2013011159

Manufactured in the United States of America
1 – BP – 7/15/13

TABLE OF CONTENTS

Chapter One

Beach Ball Relay

My name's Natalie. I'm helping my teacher, Ms. Starr, get our class ready for Field Day. I'm captain of the Beach Ball Relay!

Uh-oh. Patrick dropped the ball. He has to catch his breath. Audrey and Luis do too.

How will we ever win the race?

Ms. Starr says we need exercise. Exercise is an activity that keeps our bodies healthy.

"Our bodies have muscles," she says. "We use them to jump, walk, and roll."

Exercise makes our muscles strong.
It helps us move our **best**.

Your heart is a muscle. It's about the size of your fist. The heart has a very big job. It pumps blood to every muscle in your body. The blood carries oxygen to the muscles. Muscles need oxygen to work.

Without exercise, muscles get weak. Weak muscles wear out fast. Using them makes us tired.

"Exercise will bring back your winning spirit," says Ms. Starr.

Come on, team. Let's move!

Take a deep breath. Does that make you feel good? Your body just made endorphins. Endorphins are special chemicals that lift your mood. Your body makes lots of endorphins during exercise.

Chapter Two

Can't Catch Me!

Ms. Starr says there are three kinds of exercise. They help our bodies in different ways.

Aerobic exercise works out our lungs and heart. *Aerobic* means "with air."

Aerobic exercise is an activity that makes you breathe fast. Many aerobic exercises also make your bones stronger. Walking and running are good for your bones. So are jumping, skipping, and playing basketball.

Luis jumps rope. Audrey twirls a Hula-Hoop. Patrick starts a game of tag.

Can't catch me!

Anaerobic exercise makes our muscles strong.
Anaerobic means "without air."
Climbing and digging are anaerobic exercises.
So are sit-ups and push-ups.

Playing tug-of-war makes my muscles grow. **Heave ho!**

No matter what exercise you do, follow safety rules. Wear a helmet when riding your bike. Protect your skin by using sunscreen outdoors. Drink lots of water too. And always play in a safe place.

13

"Stretching exercises are important too," says
Ms. Starr. "They loosen tight muscles."

We touch our toes.
We bend sideways.

We twist and turn.

And we reach up high.

Today's Field Day!

Let's get moving. It's time for the Beach Ball Relay.

A healthy body needs lots of activity. Try fitting more exercise into your day. Watch less TV. Spend less time with computers and video games. Less screen time means more time for action!

Patrick runs. Luis passes the ball to Audrey.
And I race for the finish line.
We win!

Field Day is all done. But Ms. Starr says our fitness fun isn't over. Every day is made for exercise.

We can do chores at home.

We can play at the park.

We can go swimming or kick a ball.

You can exercise in any season. Rake leaves on a fall day. Make a pile, and jump in. When winter comes, sled down a snowy hill. Plant flowers and pull weeds in springtime. And splash around the pool in the summer.

Our class is staying active. We started a fitness club. **I'm Captain Fit!**

20

You can exercise too. Bounce a ball. Run a race.
Take the lead with your health!

Make a "My Exercise" Chart

Did you know that kids need at least sixty minutes of exercise each day? It's best if most of that exercise is aerobic. Be sure to include some aerobic exercises for your bones too. Anaerobic exercises are also important. Try to do them at least three times a week. And don't forget to stretch! Want to make sure you're exercising enough? Keep track of your exercise by making a "My Exercise" chart.

What you need:
a piece of paper
a pencil
a ruler

1) Turn the piece of paper on its side. At the top of the paper, write "My Exercise." Underneath, write the days of the week from left to right.

2) Along the left side of the paper, write "Exercise activities," and "Total time," from top to bottom.

3) Make rows and columns. Use a ruler and a pencil to draw straight lines from top to bottom and left to right.

4) Every day this week, try to exercise for at least sixty minutes. Write down the activities you choose for each day. Mark down how much time you spent on each activity. Then add up the times for each day's total.

5) After you finish your exercise chart, start a new one for the next week. Mix it up by choosing different activities to do. Exercising will keep you and your muscles in great shape. So don't wait. Get moving!

MY EXERCISE

	MON.	TUES.	WED.	THURS.	FRI.	SAT.	SUN.
Exercise activities	Biking (20 min.) Soccer (30 min.) Monkey bars (15 min.)	Playing tag (30 min.) Basketball (20 min.) Cleaning room (10 min.)	Gymnastics (60 min.) Sit-ups & push-ups (10 min.)				
Total time	65 minutes	60 minutes	70 minutes				

GLOSSARY

aerobic exercise: an activity that makes the heart and the lungs work hard. *Aerobic* means "with air."

anaerobic exercise: an activity that makes muscles stronger. *Anaerobic* means "without air."

exercise: an activity that a person or an animal does to stay healthy

fitness: being strong and healthy

heart: a muscle in the chest. The heart pumps blood and brings oxygen to every muscle in the body.

lungs: a pair of organs used to breathe

muscles: parts of the body that are used for movement

oxygen: a gas that most living things need to breathe. Oxygen is part of the air we breathe.

BOOKS

Bellisario, Gina. *Keep Calm: My Stress-Busting Tips.*
Minneapolis: Millbrook Press, 2014.
In this book, Anna learns that exercise is one great way to deal with stress.

Cleary, Brian P. *Run and Hike, Play and Bike: What Is a Physical Activity?*
Minneapolis: Millbrook Press, 2011.
This fun book teaches why it's important to get one hour of exercise each day.

Rockwell, Lizzy. *The Busy Body Book: A Kid's Guide to Fitness.*
Decorah, IA: Dragonfly Books, 2008.
Learn how the different parts of your body work together to keep you moving.

WEBSITES

BAM! Body and Mind
http://www.bam.gov/sub_physicalactivity/index.html
Take the Motion Commotion quiz, and find out what activities fit you best.
Learn which muscles you use for those activities too.

LERNER SOURCE™
Expand learning beyond the printed book. Download free, complementary educational resources for this book from our website, www.lerneresource.com.

Kid Exercises: 4 Types
http://fit.webmd.com/kids/move/article/exercise-types
What are some good bone-strengthening exercises? What about aerobic and anaerobic? Go to this website to find out.

Kidnetic
http://kidnetic.com/
This website is from the International Food Information Council Foundation. It has computer games that get you moving.